STUCK
ON THE
WHEEL
By S. E. McKenzie

DEDICATION
To everyone who has been left out in the cold.

THIS BOOK IS A BOOK OF SPECULATIVE FICTION
Characters, companies, governments, places, events, are either products of the author's imagination or used fictitiously. Any resemblance to persons (living or dead), companies, governments, places and/or events, is a coincidence.

TABLE OF CONTENTS

STUCK ON THE WHEEL
I

Life is round
A true circle;
A cycle

Crashes
When pedaling
Stops.

Cycles;
Boom
And bust,

Left over treasure
Piled up
To rust.

Were we born
Just to die
And turn into dust?

We carry paper
Which says
'In God we Trust."

II

What is more ruthless?
Laws of Nature
Or Military Man?

What is more truthless? Hell;
Boots marching on the ground;
Blowing up bridges all around;

As town after town
Has life
Turning upside down.

Callous and hardened
From many years of war
Frame of mind has turned unkind.

To occupy one must be willfully blind.
To live and let die
Without shedding a tear;

The occupied were immersed in all their fear.
As town after town
Destroyed themselves;

STUCK ON THE WHEEL: Because True Life Is Round

While the occupiers were marching near.

Stopped to stand on the hill,
And watched neighbor
Kill neighbor;

No longer a stranger's prisoner.
They only saw danger
In each other;

So willing to kill
Sister and brother;
So willing to kill

One another.

Before they died
At their enemy's hand;
And have their land

And home disappear;
Leaving them with no hope
Just degradation and fear.

III

Hell?
Ghosts roaming the earth
Without being able to touch or taste

All that they love;
Not yet ready to die;
Their souls could not fly

To the heavens above.

And beneath;

The scariest world of all
Is a world without Love,
Or compassion.

Being looked through
As if your mind
Was not there.

Abuse of discretionary power
Dissolving another's content
Without a care.

Manufacturing
Consent
As if a person's was not there.

IV

We never were defeated
Even though the other side
Told us that we would be better off

If we were deleted.

We would not commit suicide;
Even though what we were clinging to
Was being threatened by the enemy's acts.

The foreign police
Differentiated us;
They bigotized us;

They criticized us.
They screamed at us
To stop.

If we had
We would have
Been defeated.

We took a stand,
Never to be deleted.
We held each other's hand

And stood tall;
In the Negative Zone
Many were pushed

Into the fall;
So alone
Forever unequal;

The privileged
Felt so gleeful;
Marching boots

Echoed through the land.
We took each other's hand;
As they undervalued us;

STUCK ON THE WHEEL: Because True Life Is Round

They said
There was only one escape
For us;

The barriers went up;
As the foreign elite filled their cup;
They said our time was up.

And I knew being so unequal
Was stifling
Me and you;

What a deal for them;
What a steal;
Leaving us to beg for our next meal;

After working overtime
We all knew the crime;
And the enemy force was frightening;

The gap was widening;
Even though our spinning world
Revolved around one sun;

While the new Gestapo
Replaced
The old Gestapo.

Today, we don't think twice
We know when to run;
Nouveau Gestapo

Can't control his gun.

The idle rich accuse and abuse
All day long;
They fear that the poor

Will take over their yard.
Nouveau Gestapo stays on guard;
Plays the host;

For the library is his post;
He hears complaints day after day
That poor looking people are sitting in chairs

And are in the way;

STUCK ON THE WHEEL: Because True Life Is Round

Still clinging to the truth
Now only found
In holy books;

So dusty; along library walls;
Old society lost;
Occupiers never knew the cost;

Nouveau Gestapo
Replaced the Old Gestapo;
Too afraid of risk

To let go;
Still clinging
To books now on fire;

Nouveau Gestapo waved the poor away;
Never to be the same
Again;

For what was broken inside
Kept most afraid of the unknown.
As their chains were taken away;

They were too afraid to run;
So they stayed;
While the enemy displayed

Their weapons of war
On parade
Rewards of aggression.

They never spoke in words
We could understand;
They only spoke of oppression.

We were now under their command;
As they idled in lots
After killing every tree.

They were the Avant Guard
Of the new Parasite
Society.

Noxious fumes spread into a place called Infinity.
The air was harder to breathe;
We were now victims of their regression;

STUCK ON THE WHEEL: Because True Life Is Round

Why no one cried
When they died
We will never know;

The enemy loved
Their false ego
So its projection lived on.

We know how Nouveau Gestapo lies.
And if it wasn't for the sun
The world would be as cold

As gold;
While Unethical Legalist
Enjoyed the pain

He created for some
Mostly young;
Some went insane;

Self-fulfilling prophecy
Like the end of the world
Where common sense

Was no longer allowed.
Silently the people
Lost themselves into the crowd.

And only the birds were allowed to be free.

For Heaven had closed its door
And we were left more alone
Than we ever before.

It was hard to cope;
A stranger offered dope;
The Nouveau Gestapo's rope.

And so many had been

Bigotized;
Personal content
Wiped off the slate;

Now they were victim
Of mass hate;
They had to smile sweetly

STUCK ON THE WHEEL: Because True Life Is Round

To avoid a grizzly fate.

We avoided crashing onto the ground.
So we continued
Unbroken;

Our power
Was in self-knowledge
And that knowledge had awoken;

Our unified voice had spoken.

We were now as one;
And the collective soul
Would never die;

It lives and sleeps up in the sky.
Though we know the foe
By name;

Our motivation
Was more than just a game;
To us;

And how they laughed
As they watched us everyday;
Wishing that we would go away.

The barriers went up
One by one;
Then we knew

The processing had begun.

The rules
Written by militarized fools
Kept so many divided;

Kept power lopsided;
What was important
Was left undecided;

Opposite poles
Had collided;
While we refused to be misguided;

The pull of attraction was building;
And we would not be defeated;
We had no right to life;

Even though we refused to be deleted.

V
Time
Went on
Without a clock

STUCK ON THE WHEEL: Because True Life Is Round

But when an opportunity
Was about to knock
We had to have a door;

A place to call our own;
A home;
A place to rest our heads.

And we were bigotized;
Just like before
We refused to be deleted;

The enemy told us to stop;
But if we had
We would have been defeated.

So we held on to our dream;

Did not respond to their scream;
Even though they said they were in control;
Chaos was their ruthless boss;

For true life was round
And had to spin.
The most privileged

Had very thin skin;
And were so easy to offend;
By anyone they did not invite;

They flexed their might
To spite
Those they knew would lose a fight.

And the clique of sheik
Agreed
Anyone in need

Must not be seen
For the prosperity of the town
Would be questioned

Bringing property values down.
And the Clique of sheik
Had a hard line

Even though true life was always round
So the world could spin
Around one sun;

STUCK ON THE WHEEL: Because True Life Is Round

The wise knew how to bend
With the curve
Gave the Collective Soul

A one percent chance to mend.

Though having hard lines
Saved time
We knew their crime.

And kept the circle turning
For True Life was round
And there was no way out

Accept one;
We never lost Hope;
We said no to their dope;

Gestapo's rope;
For our world
Turned around One Sun.

And we were young; our life had just begun;
They said it was best for us
To be deleted

But we disagreed
We tried to find a way
To be freed;

We fought for our collective life;
Refused to be defeated
We kept our perspective; for we were fed

From the love above;
And the light of the sun
Gave us the energy to run;

From Big Brother who did not know

What He had done;
For the Prison State of Hate
Would determine Fate,

If Love did not grow
Before it was
Too late.

We refused to be defeated;
And we refused to be deleted;
For we were young; and our life had just begun.

STUCK ON THE WHEEL: Because True Life Is Round

Though we walked in pain
We knew we had
So much to gain

We knew;
What could not be sustained
Would self-destruct;

And equity lost
Would be the cost
For the city

With little day time economy;
And depended on the Economy of the Night
Filled with Neon Light.

Beer, guns and short term profit
Led many astray;
So stereotyped in Neon Hype;

We turned away;

So we could build synergy;
Generating energy
Before the time

Was gone.
Without a system to integrate
Social order would disintegrate.

Social disorder was the only growth industry
In the two block town;
We watched them march all around;

Pushing the most vulnerable
To the ground.
Social policy was written

"Don't let them stay around";

And then after the most vulnerable went missing
A new policy was written
By the same policy makers;

"A study has to be done
To determine why the missing were missing;"
And then the unwritten words were said;

"If the missing were found
Beat them into the ground
And turn their world upside down

STUCK ON THE WHEEL: Because True Life Is Round

So they will go missing again,
Cause we don't want them around,
So beat them into the ground."

And the truth
Would be spun
Inside Alien Nation"

By the same policy makers;

Common sense
Was not allowed;
We were better off

Lost in the crowd.

Wearing a frown
And a cross around their neck
They were in heaven

When they gave us heck.
The missing were now in the ground
Never to be found;

Social justice Policy
Never written
But understood

By the Gestapo in the Hood;
Desensitized
He never knew why

He turned a blind eye
While the young
Were turned away

Said they fell through the cracks;
Like they do every day;
Nouveau Gestapo turned a blind eye too;

Left the young to die
Hidden; within History;
Repeated Misery;

The old men
Died their hair
And went out to dance;

Before they fell asleep;
For evermore
Resting in Infinity's Tomb

Where there is always room
For the next generation
When their time has come.

Today; only the birds were free to be.

VI

Time had come and gone
Leaving us older;
Amongst new young;

Patterns of design;
If you know them
You will know your own mind.

Social Inclusion
Did not pay
For the few growth industries

Were now Social Disorder
And Global War;
Scariest World of all

Is a world without Love.

VII

Revolving door;
Push and shove;
Into a blue world without Love.

Love refused to die;
Or be broken;
And Love was in despair;

Love was never meant
To live in a world
Where so few would dare to care;

Never brave enough
To open
Their hearts

To Love;
Even though
No one

Wanted to live
In a world
Without Love.

VIII

We did not know if the sun would decay
In some hidden way;
The sun gave life;

And the sun
Shined;
In and around new life

So noble and pure;

Without the sun
Life would freeze
And Transform into death;

Frozen breath;
And no longer be
Alive or free.

To kiss you and me.

The sun held Earth
In position
While Earth

Rotated without division;
Why ask why?
It is always that way;

The effect of the sun
On everything on earth
Was a feeding cycle;

Growing the food chain
Which tied us
Together as one.

But why worry about such things?

IV
What will we repair,
In this time of despair?
Wealth accumulates;

Food Chain Politics
Run by dicks
Taking selfie-pics

Hidden in pockets;
Rockets; shape our borders
Through destruction;

STUCK ON THE WHEEL: Because True Life Is Round

Moving in a direction
We never chose;
Social order;

Has declined;
Differential treatment
To break your mind;

Differential treatment
Based on
How one was defined;

Social Disorder;
Growth industry;
See the benefactors

Rushing through the isle
In the grocery store
Without a smile;

Push and shove
In a world without love;
Fake apology

While you are left
Spread eagle on the floor
Just like the night before.

As they push you out of the way.
New social order
Threatening to close every border;

How they complain;
They expected more gain;
When they turned a blind eye

To their neighbor's pain;
So willfully blind;
They made the world less kind.

Mean girls sitting on shelves
Behind the steely watchers
Hiding their guns;

Think about it too long
It will give you the runs;
Don't let what they have done

STUCK ON THE WHEEL: Because True Life Is Round

Linger in your mind;
For your armor will protect you
For ever more;

Don't close your mind
Just close your door
And your eyes too;

For only the birds
Were really
Free to be

We had no time to reflect;
Had suffered years of neglect;
Would never be a member of the select;

Those who the system would protect;
Thin skinned;
Quick to differentiate

Between the haves and have nots;
Quick to take offence
Would treat the have-nots as worthy

Of less than two cents.
You would never be
A member of the select few;

That was true;

That is why
I love you;
I thought you knew.

For True Life
Was round;
For Spin's sake

Don't get lost
In their hard line;
Used to define

The unborn
And those
Life has torn

Now living in Infinity
For evermore
For Heaven has closed its door.

X
Hungry Bear
Caught in Apple Tree;
Bear knew it was the end.

The bullet pierced his heart
And ours too
As the mighty beast

Whimpered before he died.

XI
Concrete jungle
Would never show from below;
But when we flew above
We saw so little Love.

THE END

Bonus Poems
Excerpted from
Haunted Poems
Hunted Shadows

A CIRCLE

Was he trapped in a circle?
Or was the trap a sphere?
Whatever it was,
It was bounded by fear.

Some said chaos ruled,
Opposing forces,
Contracting, expanding,
Making the sphere spin.

No one knew how the sphere began,
A time before this conception,
Pre-programmed reception,
The collective was waiting.

As tilted poles
Were being pulled
And pushed
By a force unknown

Pressure was building,
While many were trapped inside,
This sphere of fear,
Some called a circle.

THE LINK

He asked love,
How long was forever,
And if she was
Ready to expand.

He asked love to make him stronger,
So that he could understand,
The worlds inside the Earth,
That he will never see.

He is so afraid to live,
But more afraid to die,
He asked love,
If she was just another lie.

LOST IN THE SKY

You were so proud
Held your head high
Never felt lost before
Never been thrown on the floor

Big man of the universe
It was easy to love in your omniverse
Polarized as opposites fight
Believing each one to be right

You aged with time
Forgot how to rhyme
You crumpled your paper in hand
You forgot how to take time to understand

You were not the same
And it showed
No longer big man of the universe
You complained about pain every day

Cause the pain never went away
Until you shot your head off into the wall
And faded into the sky like stardust so small
Bones buried in the ground never make a sound

For they sleep in soft satin

LEARNING

His momma held his hand
Until the task was done
Then he realized that writing
And reading could be fun

Sure he could run
And Jump sort of high,
But when he learned to read and write,
He could fly into the sky and do it all night.

He could be anything he wanted to be
Short tall, young and old.
All those doors were open to him
He could be part of the story,

And he could feel all the glory,
Cause he could do it all.
With knowledge came power,
So he never felt small.

Learning (continued)

Content inside which could only grow
Because it doesn't ever overflow
It connects to the next
And doesn't let go

Thoughts and dreams
That he could believe in.
When all was said
'I think therefore I am'

And he was then able to inspire
As reading and thinking caught fire
It was more than just a dream
It was an ideal to believe in.

His pen became the sword
That never took life.
His pen became the sword
That sought peace during strife.

BEHIND A WALL

Well he couldn't adjust
And his life was a bust
He couldn't find love

And no one could see
The sad man
Lost in the crowd

No one knew his name
Though he had everything a person could desire
But love, everything else, was not enough

He looked for a smile
And he saw no expression at all
They could not see him

For he was living behind a wall

THE END

Produced by S.E. McKenzie Productions
First Print Edition November 2015

Enquiries: 1(778)992-2453
Mailing Address:
S. E. McKenzie Productions
168 B 5ᵗʰ St.
Courtenay, BC
V9N 1J4

Email Address:
messidartha@aol.com

http://www.amazon.com/SarahMcKenzie/e/B00H9RWX48